animal attack!

RAT ATTACKS

Cynthia Laslo

HIGH
interest
books

Children's Press
A Division of Grolier Publishing
New York / London / Hong Kong / Sydney
Danbury, Connecticut

To Wanda, Steve, and Bella who provided me a nest of my own.

Book Design: Kim M. Sonsky
Contributing Editor: Jennifer Ceaser

Photo Credits: p. 5 © Bomford/Animals Animals; p. 6 © Terry Whittaker; Frank Lane Picture Agency/CO/CORBIS; p. 9 © Peter Weimann/Animals Animals; p. 11 © Stephen Dalton/Animals Animals; pp. 13, 31 © R. Redfern/Animals Animals; pp. 14, 21 © J. Downer/Animals Animals; p. 16 B & B Wells/Animals Animals; p. 18 © AP/Wide World Photos; p. 23 © Everett; p. 25 © TC Nature/Animals Animals; p. 28 © Planet Earth Pictures/FPG; p. 32 © Jeffrey L. Rotman/CORBIS; p. 35 © Uwe Walz/CORBIS; p. 37 © Steve Chenn/CORBIS; p. 38 © Telegraph Colour Library/FPG.

Visit Children's Press on the Internet at:
http://publishing.grolier.com

Library of Congress Cataloging-in-Publication Data

Laslo, Cynthia, 1943–
  Rat attacks / by Cynthia Laslo.
    p. cm.—(Animal attacks)
  Includes bibliographical references (p. 44).
  Summary: Discusses the history of rat attacks on humans and other animals as
    well as descriptions of rat species, their life cycle, and habitat.
  ISBN 0-516-23317-3 (lib. bdg.) – ISBN 0-516-23517-6 (pbk.)
    1. Rat attacks—Juvenile literature. [1. Rats.] I. Title. II Series.

QL737.R666 L36 2000
599.35—dc21

                                                                    99-058300

contents

introduction

Rats! When you think of rats, do you think of dirty animals hiding in garbage? Do you think of rats in cages being used for laboratory tests? Do you think of small and lovable pets? Rats are all of those things. They are intelligent creatures that can communicate with one another. They also can be aggressive. If they feel threatened, rats will fight to the death.

Rats have lived alongside human beings for thousands of years. Living near people meant that the rats could always find something to eat. Though you may not see them, rats are always near us. This can mean great danger for the people living near the rats!

Aside from humans themselves, rats are responsible for more human deaths than are all

Though the rat is small, it is the deadliest predator known to humankind.

other predators combined. A predator is an animal that kills other animals.

Rats have spread some of the most deadly diseases known to humankind. In the past one hundred years, more than 10 million people have died from diseases carried by rats. Rats continue to spread disease, spoil our food supplies, and occasionally, even attack helpless people.

What are these small creatures and how do they manage to do so much damage?

chapter one

A RAT'S LIFE

On August 31, 1999, an airplane was traveling from Los Angeles, California, to Auckland, New Zealand. A woman on the flight had fallen asleep. She woke up when she felt something climbing up her right leg. She lifted her blanket to see what it was. There sat a rat, right on her lap! Horrified, the woman screamed for help. The rat quickly ran to the back of the plane and hid.

When the plane landed, officials searched the plane from top to bottom. The rat was nowhere to be found. The plane had to be quarantined (put in a secure area) and sprayed with rat poison. Rats can carry many diseases that are dangerous to humans.

WHAT IS A RAT?

Rats belong to a family of animals called rodents. Other creatures in the rodent family include beavers, prairie dogs, mice, chipmunks, and gerbils. Rodents all have one amazing thing in common. Their front teeth never stop growing! Animals in the rodent family must gnaw, or chew, things to keep their teeth from growing too long. If rats didn't gnaw, their teeth would grow so long that they would not be able to close their mouths. A rat's front teeth, called incisors, can grow as much as 6 inches (15 cm) each year. In fact, if the rat didn't gnaw, its lower incisor could grow long enough to pierce its own brain.

There are more than 300 species (kinds) of rats. Most rats live in the wild. The rats most common in North America are the brown rat and the black rat.

The Brown Rat

Brown rats are known as Norway rats or common rats. They are very talented swimmers. In fact, they

Brown rats often can be found living near water.

can swim for hours and tread water for as long as three days. Brown rats often live on riverbanks and swim easily from one shore to the other. They also live in sewers and garbage dumps. Brown rats dig nests deep in the ground or in the walls of houses. A rat's nest is a warm, dark place called a burrow. Brown rats dig burrows near places where they can find food.

Brown rats have brownish-gray fur. They have small ears and short, round snouts. Brown rats have long, hairless tails and thick bodies. An adult brown rat can weigh up to 1 pound (300 to 500 grams). It can be more than 17 inches (45 cm) long. The male rat is larger than the female rat, but the female is fatter.

The Black Rat

Black rats also are called roof rats or ship rats. They are known for their excellent climbing and jumping skills. Black rats swim and burrow as do brown rats. However, they prefer high places, such as roofs, attics, and trees. They usually make their nests in these higher areas. They can scale brick walls and metal pipes to get to upper floors. They move from building to building along telephone and power lines. A black rat can even jump from rooftop to rooftop if it is being chased. They can jump as high as 3 feet (91 cm) and as far as 4 feet (121 cm).

Black rats have black or dark gray fur. They have large ears and pointed snouts. Black rats are smaller and thinner than brown rats and weigh

Black rats are excellent climbers.

about half as much. They grow to be almost a foot long (30 cm) and weigh about 10 ounces (283 g). A black rat's hairless tail is longer than its body.

A FAMILY OF RATS

Some scientists estimate that there are 6.05 billion rats in the world. That would be a few million more rats than people! How did the rat population get so big? There are two reasons. The first is that a mother rat's litter is large. As many as twelve baby rats can be born in one litter! The second reason is that rats can give birth at a very young age. At just four months old, female rats can start having babies of their own.

Newborn rats are born blind. They have no hair on their bodies for

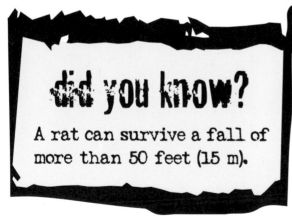

did you know?

A rat can survive a fall of more than 50 feet (15 m).

A rat can give birth to as many as twelve babies in one litter.

the first two weeks of their lives. Newborn rats are completely helpless. They must depend on their parents for food and for protection against predators. A mother rat will defend her nest and babies at any cost. Male and female rats work together to make sure that their babies are fed. Sometimes the male rats will eat less to feed the mother rats and the babies.

Rats live together in large groups called packs.

Rats are social animals that live in large groups called packs. As many as 220 rats will make up a pack. They will work together to build a connected system of burrows. The burrow system will have a strong male leader. A male rat usually becomes a leader by fighting with other rats in the burrow.

RAT APPETITES
Rats eat a third of their weight every day. Each year, a rat will eat about 50 pounds (22 kg) of

food. They gather most of their food at night. They usually travel between 100 and 150 feet (30–45 m) from their nests to look for food. Brown rats like to eat meat, fish, nuts, pet food, and insects. Black rats prefer plant foods. These include fruits, vegetables, nuts, tree bark, and seeds. However, if nothing else is available, rats will eat foods they don't normally like.

Rats, especially those living in cities, often eat human leftovers or garbage. As a result, they are sometimes faced with unfamiliar foods. When tasting new foods, a rat will take only a tiny nibble. If a rat becomes sick or dies, the other rats in the burrow will stay away from that food.

RAT HABITS

Rats spend more than half the time they are awake gnawing. Rats gnaw just about everything. A rat's top front teeth are incredibly powerful. They can chew through concrete, bricks, and steel. They gnaw floors, furniture, and plaster. By

gnawing on power lines, rats have caused blackouts in big cities. In homes and buildings, rats can cause flooding (when they chew through pipes) and fires (when they gnaw electrical wires). Rats start an estimated 5 to 25 percent of

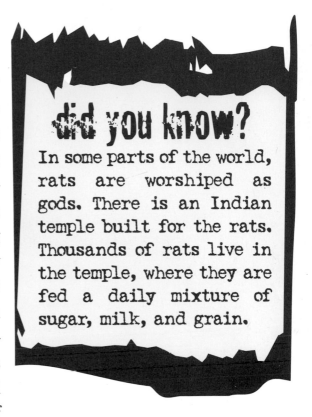

did you know?

In some parts of the world, rats are worshiped as gods. There is an Indian temple built for the rats. Thousands of rats live in the temple, where they are fed a daily mixture of sugar, milk, and grain.

all building fires. Entire buildings have collapsed because of rats' gnawing. When there is nothing to gnaw, rats will grind their own teeth.

Rats never stop gnawing.

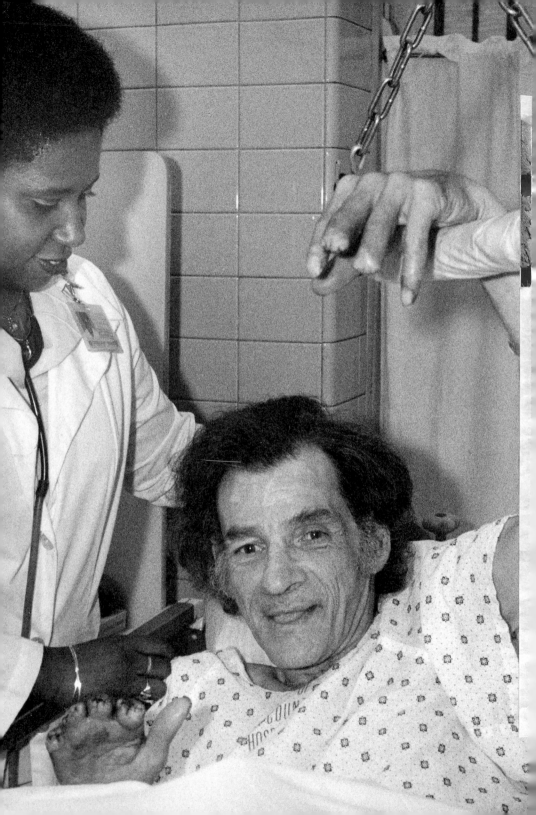

chapter two

UNDER ATTACK!

In 1979, a Chicago man named Dave Holman fell while cleaning his basement. Holman was so badly hurt that he was unable to drag himself up the stairs. Bleeding and injured, Holman attracted the attention of hungry rats. During the two weeks that he was trapped in the basement, Holman had to fight for his life against the rodents. They attacked and chewed his fingers and legs.

Holman was finally rescued and brought to the hospital. His lower legs had been horribly bitten and chewed. The rats had gnawed off almost all of his fingers. Holman's legs had to be amputated (cut off) below the knee because of infection from the rat

Rat attack survivor Dave Holman

bites. Only his thumb and index finger were left on his right hand. The doctors were able to save only three fingers on the left hand.

There are so many stories about vicious rat attacks that it is hard to know which ones are true and which ones are just scary stories. There are legends of huge armies of rats taking over entire cities in India. Make no mistake, though. Many rat stories are true. Rats can become killers when they are hungry or when their territory is being threatened.

RATS ATTACK RATS

Rats can be very aggressive creatures. Male rats will fight to the death to become leader of a burrow. If there is no food supply, rats may start eating each other. Hungry mother and father rats sometimes even eat their own babies.

A rat will attack a rat that is a stranger to its colony. A rat uses both its sharp sense of smell and certain sounds to identify whether another rat is a

Male rats will fight each other to become leader of a burrow.

friend or enemy. Rats have very poor eyesight, so they become familiar with the smell of one another's bodies and urine. One rat will smell another and then crawl under its leg. A mother rat may kill a baby rat after a human has touched it because it smells unfamiliar.

Rats also communicate with one another using high-pitched squeaks. Most of these sounds are so

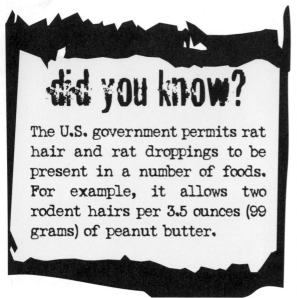

did you know?

The U.S. government permits rat hair and rat droppings to be present in a number of foods. For example, it allows two rodent hairs per 3.5 ounces (99 grams) of peanut butter.

high that human ears cannot hear them. These sounds are called ultrasonic. Rats that share a burrow can identify each other by the ultrasonic sounds they make. If a rat enters the burrow and cannot make the correct sound, it will be attacked.

ATTACKING OTHER ANIMALS

Rats are omnivores. Omnivores are animals that eat both plants and animals. Omnivores also can be predators. Rats will attack almost any animal, even an elephant! Rats will bite an elephant's trunk, leading to infection and sometimes death. Rats will eat birds, fish, and other rodents. They will gnaw their way into a henhouse and eat all the chickens and eggs. The birds are often found with

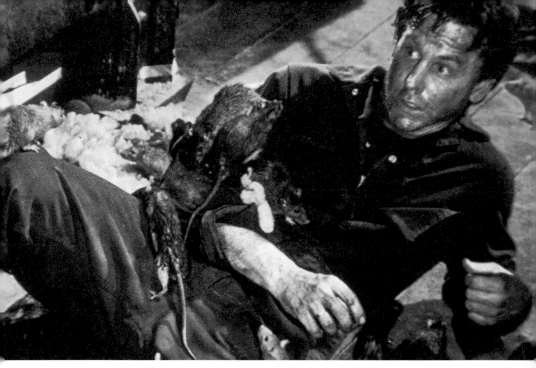

Hollywood films play on people's natural fear of rats. This is a scene from the movie *Graveyard Shift*.

just their brains or heads eaten. Rats also attack farm animals and pets. They usually will go after newborn animals, such as baby pigs and kittens.

ATTACKING HUMANS

Rats bite about 40,000 Americans every year. Worldwide, the number of people who suffer from rat bites runs into the millions. Most bites occur in large cities where humans and rats live side-by-side. Hundreds of rats may live on one city block.

RAT ATTACKS

Rats usually go after the weakest humans: old people, young children, and, particularly, babies. A human baby is unable to defend itself against a rat attack. Babies are especially at risk when they have recently had a bottle of milk to drink. A hungry rat can smell the milk on a baby's face and hands. Then the rat will climb into the crib to get a taste of the milk. It will begin biting the baby. Many babies have been eaten alive by rats as they lay helpless in their cribs.

There also are cases of rats attacking people for no good reason. In 1979, in New York City, a woman walking by an abandoned restaurant was attacked by a large group of rats. A man passing by helped the woman fight off the rats. The next day, the Department of Pest Control investigated the restaurant site. Hundreds of rat burrows were discovered in the building. Thousands of rats had to be killed. Poison was used to kill some of the rats. Others were clubbed to death with shovels or stabbed with rakes.

Many rats make their burrows in abandoned buildings.

Reports of rats attacking humans at random are rare. They are extreme examples of rat problems. Usually, rats will attack only when they are searching for food or are frightened for their safety.

RATS AS FRIENDS

In 1980, a 74-year-old woman and her daughter were found to be living in a rat-infested house in Chicago. The women treated rats as pets, even though there were hundreds of rats! The house was filled with old furniture, garbage, and newspapers. The rats made comfortable homes wherever they liked. The neighbors complained about the smell coming from the house. When the city's pest control department arrived, they found the floor covered with piles of rat droppings 3 inches (8 cm) deep!

TASTY TREAT?

In ancient times, the Romans raised rats on farms for food. During China's T'ang dynasty (A.D. 618–907), people were fond of eating baby rats stuffed with honey. During the late 1700s, when there was a food shortage in Paris, markets sold rats as meat.

Today, in Malawi, Africa, rats are eaten on a regular basis. Rats are caught and tied to sticks with string. Then the rats are roasted over a fire. They are cooked until their fur is burned off and the meat is done. Many food markets in Malawi sell rats-on-a-stick as a snack. In the Philippines, black rats are skinned and their guts are removed. Then the rats are deep-fried in oil. Many people have described rat meat as being very tender and tasting of almonds.

chapter three

RATS AND DISEASE

Many of us think of rats as dirty animals that are covered with germs. This is true, but it is because rats spend so much time in contact with human garbage and waste. Rats actually have very clean habits. Rats enjoy water and wash themselves whenever they can. Like cats, rats clean themselves by licking their paws and brushing other parts of their bodies. However, even the cleanest rats can carry diseases. Many of these diseases are deadly.

THE BLACK PLAGUE

The Black Death (also called bubonic plague) was a fatal disease that killed more than 75 million

Rats can pass diseases to humans by coming into contact with our food, such as grain.

people worldwide between the 1300s and the 1700s. Europe lost one fourth of its entire population to the Black Death. The rats themselves did not cause the disease. However, they did carry fleas and lice on their bodies. The fleas and lice were infected with the germs that caused the plague. People caught the plague when these insects bit them. People also became ill after eating food with which rats had come in contact.

The Black Death continued to spread from person to person as they coughed. Symptoms of plague were swelling in the groin and armpits. This was followed by a rash of purple and black spots all over the body. Death soon followed. There was no cure.

There have been smaller outbreaks of the plague ever since. In 1994, several hundred people died in India from plague. As recently as 1997, there were plague infections in Africa. Fortunately, plague can now be treated if it is caught early enough. If a person infected with plague is not treated in time, he or she certainly will die.

OTHER DISEASES

Rats carry more than thirty-five diseases that can be dangerous, or even fatal, to humans. Diseases can be transmitted (given) to humans directly from a rat

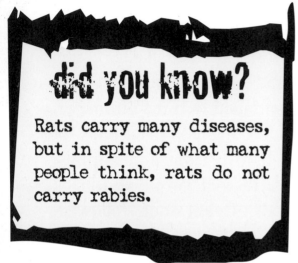

did you know?

Rats carry many diseases, but in spite of what many people think, rats do not carry rabies.

bite. People also can catch diseases from rat-contaminated food. Fleas and lice may bite an infected rat and then bite a person. That person may then catch the disease the rat is carrying. The following are just two of the diseases carried by rats and transmitted to humans.

Rat-Bite Fever

Rat-bite fever is transmitted directly to humans through a rat bite. Only a small number of people who are bitten by a rat will catch the disease. The disease is carried in the teeth and gums of many rats. People who have rat-bite fever have many of the same symptoms as the flu. Rat-bite fever can be treated, but it can cause death in babies and elderly people.

Rats can carry the disease salmonella, which causes food poisoning.

Salmonella

Salmonella is a type of bacteria that causes infection in a person's intestines. It is the most common cause of food poisoning. Salmonella bacteria is found in sewers, garbage, and places where there is rotting food. These are the same areas where rats like to hang out. Many rats become infected with salmonella. They transmit it to humans when their droppings come in contact with dishes, silverware, countertops, or food.

ZINC PHOSPHIDE TECH.
COMMANDO

Reg. No. 5-4

NET WT.

HOUSE

Keep out of reach of children. If swallowed or if symptoms occur, call physician immediately.

जहर विष
POISON

बच्चों की पहुँच से दूर रखिये यदि जहर निगल लिया हो या जहर के लक्षण दिखाई दे तो डॉक्टर को तुरन्त बुलाइयो।

मुलांपासून दूर ठेवा
जर गिळले गेले असल्यास अथवा विषबाधा झाल्याची लक्षणे दिसत्यास त्वरीत डॉक्टराना बोलवा.

ANTIDOTE: SYM Symptoms are n and abdominal p and neurological lead to death.

FIRST AID: Indu a tablespoon of Repeat treatment

DRUG THERAPY 1:5000 Potassium Cupric Sulphate an emetic. Gener including adminis control haemorrh the patient with recommended.

Active ingredient:
Zinc Phosphide 80% w/w Min.

Inert ingredient: 20% w/w Max.

Zinc Phosphide is to kill rats.
Toxicity - Acute oral (rat) LD 50:45.7 mg/kg.

DIRECTION FOR USE: Mix 10 gms of Zinc Phosphide with 10 gms of edible oil and then mix with 380 gms of food material. Keep 10 gms. of poisoned bait at each baiting station.

PRECAUTIONS: Highly toxic. Do not inhale dust and fumes. Keep material and baits away from domestic animals, food stuff and empty food stuff containers. Keep it in packed dry condition. Never use water instead of oil while mixing. Remove & bury all baiting residues & dead animals.

STORAGE & DISPOSA Keep in almirahs und carefully before use

FOR AGRICULTU जिंक फॉस्फाइड चूहें का म विष्लाम : (चूहे के) खाने ग्राम/कि. ग्राम

 Manufactured by:
EXCEL INDUSTRIES LIMITED
Regd. Office: 184/87, S.V. Road, Jogeshwari,
Bombay-400 102. Manufactured at Bombay-400 058.

chapter four

FIGHTING BACK

It is clear that humans have very real reasons to be worried about rats. Rats damage food supplies and property. Scientists estimate that rats destroy about 20 percent of the world's food supply each year. Rats carry diseases that are dangerous and sometimes deadly. Their bites can badly injure and even kill people and other animals. Rats are one of man's most harmful enemies.

How do human beings fight against rats? It is not easy. Rats are smart creatures. They have learned to avoid poison and other methods humans use to kill them.

One method of killing rats is to use poison.

RAT ATTACKS

Poison

Killing rats is not easy. Exterminators have used different kinds of rat poison over the years. In fact, scientists have found some rats that have grown resistant to poison. This means that the rats have gotten used to poison and can't be harmed by it. These rats, called super rats, can survive even if given one hundred times the amount of poison it takes to kill a normal rat.

It is also very difficult to get rats to eat poison. Rats are very afraid of eating food with which they are not familiar. If one rat dies from poisoning, the other rats in a burrow will be careful not to make the same mistake.

If a rat is tricked into eating poison, it usually dies. A rat does not have the ability to vomit to get the poison out of its body.

Traps

There are a number of different kinds of rat traps. The most common are snap traps and glue traps.

Some people set traps to kill bothersome rats.

Snap traps use bait, such as peanut butter or bacon, to lure rats to the trap. When a rat shows up to investigate the food, it touches a trigger that snaps the trap shut. Usually the trap snaps shut on the rat's head or crushes its back. Snap traps usually kill the rat quickly so it doesn't suffer.

Glue traps also are baited with food. When the rat gets near the bait, its feet get caught in a sticky material. Often rats will struggle violently when they become stuck. As they struggle, other body parts stick to the trap. Glue traps are a terrible way for rats to die. They may get their noses stuck in glue while they struggle. Then they suffocate (die from lack of air). Some rats have been known to chew off their own legs to get free of a glue trap.

Unique Methods

Poison alone often is not enough to kill rats. In Bombay, India, there are four times as many rats as there are people. There are reports that four thousand rats are killed each night in Bombay. However, poison kills only about half of the rats. People roam the streets at night and kill about two thousand rats a night by clubbing them to death. In the Philippines, groups of people use flame-throwers to set fire to the rats' burrows.

OUR FRIEND, THE RAT

Although rats have proven to be a danger to humans, they also have helped us. Without rats,

Scientists perform tests on rats to help discover and treat diseases in humans.

scientists would not be able to test many of the medicines that have saved human lives. Even the National Institute of Health has stated that rats are necessary to help scientists discover the cause of many human diseases. Rats also have helped scientists to figure out treatments or cures for many of those diseases.

Many people also enjoy keeping a rat as a pet. They can be very affectionate creatures. Male rats like to have their ears scratched by their owners. Female rats like to play games.

did you know?

Dogs make better rat catchers than do cats. Dogs are less afraid of the rodents than are cats.

Rats have lived side-by-side with human beings for centuries. They have survived plagues, poisons, traps, and much more. Humans have been unable to invent anything that will rid the world of rats. It looks as though rats are here to stay.

Some people like to keep rats as pets.

FACT SHEET

Rattus norvegicus Scientific name for the brown rat
(also called Norway rat or common rat)

Rattus rattus Scientific name for the black rat
(also called ship rat or roof rat)

Life Span
Average life span for rats: 1 to 3 years

Life Cycle
Baby rats born 21 days after conception.
Baby rats weaned at 22 days.
Rats can mate 80 days after they've been weaned.
Old age is considered 15 months.
A female rat has an average of 22 babies in
her lifetime.

Number of young per litter
Brown rat   8-10
Black rat   4-8
Number of litters each year
Brown rat   3-7
Black rat   3-9

Distribution of rats in North and South America

Black Rat   Brown Rat

new words

bubonic plague (also called the Black Death) a deadly disease that spread from flea-infested rats to humans during the Middle Ages; occasional outbreaks of this disease still occur

burrow a rat's shelter (noun); to dig to make a shelter (verb)

contaminate to infect by coming into contact; especially with food

dynasty a powerful family that rules for a long time

exterminator someone who gets rid of household pests, usually by killing them

germ a tiny organism that can cause disease

gnaw to bite or chew on with the teeth

incisor a front tooth used for cutting

litter the offspring of an animal that has multiple births in one delivery

omnivore an animal that eats both plants and animals

pack a group of rats that live together

plague see bubonic plague

predator an animal that hunts and kills other animals

rodent a small, gnawing mammal

salmonella a kind of bacteria that causes food poisoning

snout nose of an animal

territory an area that is occupied and defended by an animal or group of animals

ultrasonic having a sound frequency that is too high for human ears to hear

wean when a mother stops giving a baby her milk

for further reading

Alderton, David. *Rodents of the World.* New York: Facts on File, Inc., 1996.

Daly, Carol Himsel. *Rats: A Complete Pet Owner's Manual.* Hauppauge, NY: Barron's Educational Series, 1991.

Hendrickson, Robert. *More Cunning Than Man.* New York: Kensington Books, 1983.

resources

Animal Attack Files

http://www.igorilla.com/gorilla/animal/

This site offers a great selection of news articles describing recent attacks on humans by animals. Included is a link to book lists for further reading.

Animal Diversity Web

http://animaldiversity.ummz.umich.edu/index.html

Includes an index where you can search for the Norway rat, the black rat, or any other mammal. Presents the history of rats as well as giving information about rat characteristics and habits.

Discovery Online: Black Death

www.discovery.com/stories/history/blackdeath/blackdeath.html

Explore one of the world's worst epidemics. Click on the rat and follow its journey as it spreads the bubonic plague across Asia, Europe, and Great Britain. Includes accounts of the plague as well as illustrations.

Rat and Mouse Club of America

www.rmca.org

Information about owning rats and mice as pets. Includes general information about rats, photos, a rat magazine, and outlines how to become a club member.

Squeak! Magazine

www.chirpy.com/squeak/

An online magazine about pet rats. Discusses rat care and includes photos, stories, and links to rat clubs.

index

About the Author

Cynthia Laslo was born in Norway and moved to Iowa with her parents in 1955. After high school, she taught English as a second language in the school system of Maricao, Puerto Rico. She now lives in Pearl River, NY.